photo by Bill Smith

Mel Lawson

Haiku
Adventures in Verse

Mel Lawson

For Joan ~ who will [mixed?] by all who had the good fortune to know her in Sacramento ~ very sincerely

Limited Edition

No. **257**   *Mel Lawson*

2/22/96

Other Books by Mel Lawson

Verse
My Gypsy Mind   1975
Word Pictures   1976
Selected Parables in Verse   1977
Scattered Leaves   1981
Uptwist   1983
Eighth Notes   1987

History
Our America: Today and Yesterday   1938
Saga of Service   1986
Flower Power   1989

ISBN 0-943787-06-8

Lawson, Mel, 1907-
Haiku
Adventures in Verse
1. Title
1991

HIBISCUS PRESS
P.O. Box 22248
Sacramento, California 95822
Current edition last digit shown 9-8-7-6-5-4-3-2-1

Contents

Prefatory Note

The haiku is one of the two major forms of poetry in Japanese literature. The other is the tanka. Both are unrhymed verses, originally linking nature and human nature. The haiku usually consists of three lines containing seventeen syllables, five in the first line, seven in the second, and five in the third. The form often is suggestive rather than definitive, a whisper rather than a shout. The early haiku had no title, no punctuation, and no required meter. Japanese is an unstressed language.

According to students the original haiku was usually serious, but at times "very funny," and the humor could be "more than a little indecent."[1]

Haiku means "opening phrase" and sprang from the tanka, which is an unrhymed Japanese poem of five lines, and a total of thirty-one syllables. The offspring was weaned from its forbear and popularized as a separate form in the Middle Ages. Its length is short, its grammar "often fragmentary," and its lines frequently broken. Forms also appear under the title hokku (the original name) and haikai.

It is impossible to produce an English haiku that duplicates the equivalent of the Japanese wordings, so different are the two languages. The English haiku is at best a loose approximation. Some writers and translators take liberties with the number of lines and syllables, but numerous critics contend that the 5-7-5, three-line treatment is best.

For the purist, no claim is made that the verses found in this book approach the gentle, fragile beauty of the original haiku or its various translations. An effort has been made to utilize the three-line seventeen-syllable form to express ideas, make observations, and point up philosophical concepts through this condensed-message medium. Thus leeway has been taken in the choice and type of topics presented.

[1] *The New Catholic Encyclopedia*, McGraw Hill Co., New York, 1967, Vol. VII, p. 851.

The secret of the haiku-form's charm lies in its simplicity and brevity. The English form was adapted "by the Imagists and other Western writers . . . who rebelled against the exuberance and sentimentality of 19th century verse."[1] Such writers as Ezra Pound, Amy Lowell, Hilda Doolittle, and Richard Aldington were attracted to the form in their quest to develop "a hard, clean, concentrated poetry free from artificialities and replete with specific physical analogies."[2]

There are no great epics or didactic poems in the Japanese language, but it has been said that perhaps the most original form of Japanese literature was poetry, and that love of country and appreciation for beauty are characteristic of its content. Possibly the most perceptive observation on Japanese versification was made by Ki no Tsurayuki in 905 A.D., when he wrote: "Japanese poetry has for its seed the human heart, and grows into countless leaves of words."[3]

In any event the haiku form is a particularly unique, delightful, and challenging vehicle for the expression of thought. As such it is most profitably read in small portions at a time, and used as a stimulus for reflective thinking.

Mel Lawson
August 1991

---

[1] *The Concise Columbia Encyclopedia*, Columbia University Press, New York, 1983, p. 402.
[2] *Ibid.*
[3] Keene, Donald, *From Japanese Literature, An Introduction for Western Readers*, Grove Press, Inc., New York, 1955, p. 22.

Acknowledgments

Thanks and appreciation from the author to the following:

Summie R. Boehm, librarian, Sacramento High School, for books and other materials on the haiku and Japanese literature.

Staff members of the California State Library.

Ruth de Polo, Robert N. Hansen, Blanche Lawson, Maridel Salisbury, and Dr. Robert S. Romeis for proofreading the original manuscript, and offering helpful suggestions.

Margaret Wensrich for Editorial Services.

Toast

Salute to haiku
The seventeen syllable
Japanese verse form.

1

Because it is brief
The song sung in a haiku
Cannot waste a word.

2

Sleep — the gift of gods
That unyokes the weight of care
And silences pain.

3

Lies travel by jet.
Truth follows on a snail's back
Seldom catching up.

4

To make life complete
After it was created
God gave man music.

5

Thoughts are companions
To be chosen with caution
Lest they undo you.

6

The spider of war
Quickly fashions a cobweb
That imprisons truth.

7

He was a rebel
Against mold and tradition.
A foe of restraint.

8

Music is language
That everyone understands
Without being taught.

9

Bells from steeples peal;
Whistles blow and dreams are real;
All because of you.

10

Spring unlocks the bud
And bids it spread its perfume
On an eager air.

11

A summer sunset
Taxes the creativeness
Of Nature's paint brush.

12

Springtime has arrived
When night is punctuated
By the cricket's chirp.

13

March evenings are marked
By the dance of the fireflies
And hoarse songs of frogs.

14

Fine poetry comes
From those who drain life's full cup
And pronounce it good.

15

When one is in love
There is nothing out of reach
Even distant stars.

16

Faith is the candle
That lightens the journey to
The impossible.

17

Listen to silence.
Its voice has a potency
That dwarfs spoken words.

18

The sighing pine tree
Has its sibling counterpart
In the human heart.

19

Hers was the good life
Spent in gathering moonbeams
And reaching for stars.

20

Truth — the fugitive
Refuses to be captured
Except in fragments.

21

The rosebud's fragrance
Hums a lovely melody
That ripples the heart.

22

Thoughts can be heightened
By contemplating the stars
And walking with trees.

23

Rainbows never last
But the fact that they appear
Tells what might have been.

24

The mind stands in awe
When one sees fragile blossoms
Dissecting a rock.

25

Those who instruct youth
Pass on the baton of life
And are forgotten.

26

You may not give much
But a thread casts a shadow
That meets someone's need.

27

Today a whisper
In Kyoto can be heard
In Tallahassee.

28

It is not the pace
But the direction followed
That insures progress.

29

Highly vocal winds
Claw at the features of a
Scowling winter sky.

30

Old wine and old friends
Give the past brighter garments
Than in fact it wore.

31

Three visual gems:
High flying geese, a cresting
Wave, an infant's smile.

32

Who is my neighbor?
The answer never changes.
Anyone in need.

33

I love the quiet
Of the lazy mellow dusk
When the world stands still.

34

We seem worlds apart
Until we sing together
And hearts are blended.

35

We may be strangers
But when we share our thinking
We fashion a bridge.

36

The Horseman of War
Seems always in the saddle.
Time he was grounded.

37

Flowers unlock hearts
Especially red roses
Which first opened yours.

38

Like an autumn frost
Teenage love evaporates
In the morning sun.

39

A waterfall sings
Of its modest origin
And quest for the sea.

40

A white polka dot
Against the sea's blue apron —
Sailboat in the sun.

41

It is hard to hate
Or find fault with one's neighbor
When his lilacs bloom.

42

A silk dress rustles
Like well-ripened autumn leaves
Blown by a soft wind.

43

After creating
The exquisite camellia
Dame Nature rested.

44

Eventide. The hour
The sun rouges the sky's cheek
Before retiring.

45

Flowers are not mute;
They are most articulate
Were we but attuned.

46

Why is it that God
In his infinite wisdom
Made autumn so brief?

47

Love knows no color,
Wears every kind of vestment,
And speaks in all tongues.

48

Roll, restless ocean.
Despite countless man-made wounds
No scar mars your face.

49

To go back in time
One must recognize the myths
That once were believed.

50

Revenge is not sweet.
It is a bitter nectar
That poisons the soul.

51

A cold stormy night
Puts the imagination
On a witch's broom.

52

Parking lot. Modern
Hitching post where metal steeds
Await their riders.

53

We are all ballots
Cast and counted every day
For what we believe.

54

Milk-white summer clouds
Form temporary islands
In a sea-blue sky.

55

Death, King of Tyrants,
Heeds no plea for clemency
Once he has decreed.

56

A woman delights
In the constant assurance
That she is much-loved.

57

Someone to hold me
When I am spent with the weight
Of this world. I need.

58

The flowering peach
One of Nature's corsages
Worn in early spring.

59

I cannot describe
In seventeen syllables
How much I love you.

60

Most fast flowing streams
Pause at frequent intervals
To form placid pools.

61

The environment
Cries out for understanding
And gentler treatment.

62

An earthquake's power
In the space of few moments
Makes people equal.

63

How many Wise Men
Brought their gifts to Bethlehem?
Scripture does not say.

64

If I said that I
Loved the winter's sullen sky
It would be a lie.[1]

65

When you are absent
I am like an empty nest
or a waveless sea.

[1] The traditional haiku is unrhymed, but the author could not resist this exception.

66

Candlelight flatters
The already beautiful
Features of women.

67

When man has freedom
He has power to forego
That which he has won.

68

How long, Lord, how long
Will the voice of the people
Be a mere whisper?

69

Of all nature's scents
What perfume is sweeter than
The fragrance of spring?

70

Life writes on the face
Of the saint and the sinner
The lines each has earned.

71

Few feats of nature
Can equal the majesty
Of blue-white glaciers.

72

She is delightful
But as elusive as a
Silhouette in smoke.

73

Nature gives strange gifts:
To the elephant, a trunk;
To a camel, humps.

74

Sweet is the music
Of the laughter of children
And pattering rain.

75

Bees are bold burglars
That invade floral castles
With intent to steal.

76

To the hummingbird
The flower is a chalice
Of candied nectar.

77

An oriole's song
And a woodpecker's drumbeat
Welcome the sunrise.

78

All the world's people
Are not on the same level
Of thinking. Thus wars.

79

A war is not won
If battleground victories
Is all it achieved.

80

Men used to whistle
While they worked. Today the sound
Is seldom heard. Why?

81

Flowers and children
Have something in common. Both
Respond to kindness.

82

Ebbing September
Continues a climate that
Holds summer hostage.[1]

83

The moon and the stars
Know that their reign has ended
When a rooster crows.

84

I improve each year;
And feel better every day;
But I fracture truth.

85

A safe prediction:
The next pope to be chosen
Will be Catholic.

[1] In the northern hemisphere.

86

Failure stands in wait
If one thinks today's success
Insures tomorrow's.

87

His world is so small
It requires only one look
To see all of it.

88

Big jobs are postponed
Because the many small ones
Consume all our time.

89

A rainbow suggests
There is yet another world
That surpasses ours.

90

Upon retirement
He learned how to do nothing
And now does it well.

91

I weigh but an ounce,
But perhaps my tiny bit
May tip the balance.

92

Winter is a guest
Unwelcome and unwanted
That must be endured.

93

What price ambition?
When the summit has been won
One feels so lonely.

94

Some minds are like moons
Without a light of their own
They merely reflect.

95

Were there no music
Life would become vapid — an
Endured existence.

96

Dreams are strange dramas
Played upon the stage of sleep
By a confused cast.

97

Two old magicians
Who can mesmerize lovers:
Moonlight and music.

98

History is Man's
Best memory of himself —
Sometimes fanciful.

99

For those who seek change
The burden of persuasion
Rests on the plaintiff.

100

Man is a tenant
Who wastes the precious treasures
Of Earth's virgin turf.

101

What songs bring more joy
To the hearts of the faithful
Than Christmas carols?

102

Poppies told of gold
In sun-kissed California
Long before Marshall.

103

Spring is a coquette;
Some days it encourages
And some days repels.

104

The date on a crypt
Does not always truly tell
When the person died.

105

Success in marriage
Can be achieved by knowing
What to overlook.

106

The Easter message
Can be explained in one word
Spelled H-O-P-E.

107

Sleep is death's sibling,
But a counterpart that is
Not so demanding.

108

Truth is not revealed
By peals of thunderous words
But by quiet thoughts.

109

From a caravan
Sound the chime of camel bells
Tinkling in the night.

110

Pundits may debate
Which came first, egg or the chick?
Do we need to know?

111

Man is a spendthrift
Who squanders the legacy
Nature has bequeathed.

112

You may become blind
But do not let sightless eyes
Rob you of vision.

113

When hens lay their eggs
Their cackle gives the action
More than it deserves.

114

Spring makes its entrance
When insects hum at sundown
And larks sing at dawn.

115

Falling autumn leaves
Like red and amber snowflakes
Give their hues to earth.

116

If I could write a
Love song for you — I would, and
Sing it if I could.

117

Wings of butterflies
Seem fragile as a cobweb
Yet they fly the wind.

118

The spent tide forsakes
Its blue, and leaves on the shore
A fringe of white lace.

119

Salmon swim upstream
Against forbidding currents
To spawn eggs and die.

120

December seventh
Nineteen hundred forty-one
The day the Dove cried.

121

Heaven is not won
By performing goodly deeds
But by endless faith.

122

Life can be so frail
That even one small puff will
Snuff out its candle.

123

The worm is at risk
When a blue jay whets his bill
On a withered bough.

124

Should one seek eagles
He must fix his eyes on crags
Where the eagles live.

125

Bubbles in the wine
Like a flirtatious woman
Suggest a promise.

126

Strange is nature. The
Ruthless avalanche is formed
By gentle snowflakes.

127

High-flying mallards
Resemble fighter squadrons
But without their guns.

128

Modern homes appeal
But often lack the charm of
A white picket fence.

129

Monarch butterflies
Add a touch of opulence
To blooms visited.

130

Wide-winged gooney birds
Perch on jagged coral reefs
But not at high tide.

131

In the midst of life
The silent Horseman of Death
Selects his victims.

132

On a tree's dead limb
A chicken hawk sits waiting
With sharp curved talons.

133

Coarse winds rasp their way
Across fields of ripened grain
Begging for harvest.

134

Mother Earth watches
As one by one her children
Are ravished by Man.

135

Sweaters must be worn
By healthy growing youngsters
When mother feels cold.

136

History ignored
Means history repeated:
A painful lesson.

137

Crows do not hurry,
That may be why they are known
As sagacious birds.

138

The flag of Japan
Signifies that each day is
A new beginning.

139

A big-billed puffin
Calmly rides a glacier chunk
In its search for food.

140

A woman's handbag:
Never has so little space
Been so sorely taxed.

141

A gray sullen sky
Reveals a lone duck's struggle
Against a raw wind.

142

Pray not to be served
But for opportunities
To be of service.

143

Even rainbows pale
When the vain, courting peacock
Flaunts his gaudy fan.

144

From the passing cloud
Earth knows both light and shadow
And a change of mood.

145

As we grow older
Tomorrows arrive faster
and days leave sooner.

146

The birth of triplets
Signifies a mother who
Exceeds instructions.

147

Immortal Shelley
Who wrote with pen borrowed from
The Muse Euterpe.

148

You give me a high
That surpasses any drug.
Is this feeling love?

149

Caravans of dreams
Cross the sands of memory
When I hear our song.

150

The mad dogs of war
Are held at bay by collars
Tissue-paper thin.

151

Lake Tahoe: gem of
The high Sierra's showcase.
Sapphire in the sun.

152

When sleep escapes you
Do not waste your time on sheep;
Review your blessings.

153

So close to love is
Music, composers seldom
Fashion songs of hate.

154

Clouds are like people.
They weep, frown, drift and grumble,
Have their hour and pass.

155

Spring comes center stage
When red robins mate and nest;
And camellias bloom.

156

From out of the depths
Of a thick awesome silence
A laughing loon calls.

157

The pale gray-white trunk
Of the tall eucalyptus
Looms ghostlike at night.

158

The lion and lamb
Lie down together till the
Lion gets hungry.

159

A single sparrow
Perched high on a power line
Watches the traffic.

160

Sing me a color
That is chosen at random
From morning's sunrise.

161

The whippoorwill's song
Is a message of sorrow
Delivered at night.

162

A raw winter wind
Huddles sparrows and linnets
On ledges and sills.

163

Smiles come in all hues;
Speak a universal tongue;
And have no accent.

164

Sometimes stone silence
Delivers stern messages
Better than language.

165

World! So big are you;
So small am I. How can I
Ever hope to cope?

166

When the heart is hurt
The tongue cannot find language
To describe the pain.

167

With the setting sun
Comes the musical magic
Of old mission bells.

168

Wars are never fought
According to agreements
Previously wrought.

169

Exhilarating
Is the garden's sweet perfume
When gardenias bloom.

170

An Indian tale
Claims that petals of poppies
Brought gold to the West.

171

Today's world awaits
The strong voice of a leader.
Someone with vision.

172

Twice martyrs know stones;
Once as deadly missiles hurled;
Once as monuments.

173

The murmur of bells
Calls the faithful to worship
In pagoda shrines.

174

The words the stars write
On night's blackboard are erased
By the morning sun.

175

Constant as waves that
Curve and crash upon the shore
Is my love for you.

176

There is a need for
An eleventh commandment:
Preserve Our Planet.

177

New worlds still exist
Awaiting modern Vikings
To discover them.

178

Roiled, surly sea-waves,
Streaked with viscous tanker oil,
Soil sandy beaches.

179

Rose petals offer
Soft landing cups for moonbeams
On their trips to Earth.

180

The stout winds of change
Keep buffeting old beliefs,
Leaving few intact.

181

The flamboyant tree
Holds up its red parasol
To tame tropic heat.

182

A blurred red ribbon
Spanning two trees . . . flight of a
Scarlet tanager.

183

Baldness in a man
Augments his face and extends
The breadth of his smile.

184

Orange-breasted robins
Love green lawns and fruit trees
While whistling their songs.

185

The scavenger gull
Contradicts its neat grooming
By gobbling garbage.

186

A pond lily floats
On a quiet garden pool
Unnoted, unsung.

187

Many third stringers
Become All-Americans
Fifty years later.

188

A bikini brief:
Seldom does so much depend
Upon so little.

189

Paradise varies.
For the bee it is clover
Blooming in the spring.

190

Good poetry is
Rhythmical language that stirs
Thought and emotion.

191

On the map of life
It is sad to see someone
Become an island.

192

Wars once prompted songs.
Now they are not regarded
As cause for singing.

193

To grow a redwood
Takes a few thousand Earth-years.
To fell it — a day.

194

You are beauty-framed.
A picture I would describe
If I had the words.

195

Two ways to drink life:
Sip it as rare vintage wine;
Gulp it down as beer.

196

A luxury ship . . .
A beaded dress. Candlelight . . .
Night to remember.

197

Comets: Thespians
That play on Earth's great sky-stage
And quickly exit.

198

Some people's fare is
The crumbs of life, while others
Enjoy its desserts.

199

The constellations
Show the residents of space
In twelve stage settings.

200

Mere proximity
Does not make one a neighbor.
Loving-kindness does.

201

Ours is a strange world.
Amid glut we have famine;
Preach peace yet wage war.

202

The Christmas story
Best can be told by the tongues
Of singing children.

203

Like sparkling red wine
Her lips were inviting and
Intoxicating.

204

One of Nature's boons
Is the rose-purple heather
And its soft fragrance.

205

Sleep, the fugitive
That some nights eludes capture
By its pursuer.

206

What matches the spell
Of a tropical beach and
A daffodil moon?

207

The voice of Error
Booms across the footlights while
Truth whispers its lines.

208

Somehow life's burdens
Seem easier to bear in
Apple blossom time.

209

Life's meaning. Is it
A phantom stalked endlessly
And never captured?

210

Tulips lift their cups
To witness bomb-laden jets
Roar to their targets.

211

Deliver us Lord
From the wisdom of people
With straightjacket minds.

212

While others write books
To inspire peoples' thinking
Let me teach their young.

213

The sirens' shrill whine
Shriek of death from the cargoes
Of high flying jets.

214

Today the art of
Patient waiting has been lost;
We want answers now.

215

Life gives no blank checks;
Live like today is your last;
Possibly it is.

216

A prayer, to be heard,
Need not be loud. God can hear
The faintest whisper.

217

Some lives resemble
Carousels turning round and
Round going nowhere.

218

A smile is silent
But its message speaks louder
Than a hundred words.

219

Peaks were made to climb,
Rivers to be bridged; and the
Oceans to be plumbed.

220

The poultice of sleep
Heals the soreness and fatigue
That each day inflicts.

221

Blue has many shades
Light and dark and in-between.
Then the best — your eyes.

222

Sunshine — gift of gifts.
Without which life could not be
Nor would the moon glow.

223

The truth and legend
Are so closely intertwined
History is rigged.

224

A lavender sky;
A blue moon; a crimson sun;
Surrealism.

225

Reverie island
Flecked with white hibiscus and
Red bougainvillea.

226

Four luminous stars
Form the awesome Southern Cross
Crowning the South Seas.

227

In the realm of IF
We are prone to speculate
On what might have been.

228

The song that I hear
Rides the wings of the night wind
And escapes capture.

229

The star-specked heavens
Suggest galaxies unseen
And worlds yet unknown.

230

Once exploration
Was for earth-bound things. Now it
Is for galaxies.

231

The chrysanthemum
Adds a glamorous mystique
To the fall season.

232

There can be no spring
Without robins and rainbows
And couples in love.

233

U.S.A. — Fifty
Red leaves held together by
A blue and white thread.

234

Two clues to autumn:
The saffron heads of plump grain
And sweet ripened grapes.

235

Winter's icy breath
Makes many birds pouters and
Silences their songs.

236

The cast-off cookie
Dismembered by tiny ants
Working in silence.

237

The faint contrail of
Fragrance left behind by a
Beautiful lady.

238

Wildlife in winter
Emigrates or hibernates
For its survival.

239

Truth is an outlaw
Forever to be hunted
But never captured.

240

A necklace of jade
Displayed on a sapphire quilt
Mirrors Hawaii.

241

Peace is so fragile —
Its future at the mercy
Of an attitude.

242

Love defies measure.
It cannot be budgeted
Or given limits.

243

A lover's heartbeat
Deviates from the normal.
Its rate is faster.

244

The daydreamer builds
Grand mansions in the sky and
Castles in the sand.

245

The meaning of dreams
Continues an enigma
To scribes and scholars.

246

Happiness has wings
That fly its joyful feeling
To deserving hearts.

247

Night's indigo blue
Plus its honey-colored stars
Adds an amber moon.

248

In the hush of dawn
Come the loud flute-like phrases
And trill of the thrush.

249

Larks sing best at dawn
But few people are awake
To hear their message.

250

A withered orchid
In an old tear-stained letter .
A shattered romance.

251

The song of the sea
With its throbbing crescendo
Sings a grand anthem.

252

Cathedral steeples
Are reminders of the fact
That life has purpose.

253

Spring is the tenor
In Earth's quartet of seasons,
Its high notes of song.

254

Life tells its secrets
To those with the courage to
Keep on wondering.

255

Alaska. Where green
Forests edge the cold blue sea
And white glaciers calve.

256

The speech was so poor
The audience gave it a
Kneeling ovation.

257

The Himalayas
Where Earth stands on tiptoe and
Whispers to the sky.

258

Seek enlightenment
For with it comes compassion
And love for mankind.

259

The desert's silence
Is so complete and heavy
It is audible.

260

The brain weighs ounces
Yet it reaches out to stars
And probes galaxies.

261

Golden-hued jonquils
Hosting yellow butterflies
In the morning sun.

262

A gentle answer
To an abrasive question
Shows maturity.

263

From a peach-tree branch
A jay vents his invective
On all bystanders.

264

Death is part of life,
An ingredient decreed
By the fact of birth.

265

Some day the sun will
Lose its light; become stone-cold;
But not in our time.

266

Blue waves rhythmically
Rushing to a sandy beach
Rimming it with foam.

267

Courage is not just
Daring. It is to live with
Endless pain and smile.

268

One gets perspective
By viewing the Milky Way
On a cloudless night.

269

Rhythmic is the beat
Of the surging silver surf
As it seeks the shore.

270

Strive for thoughts that lift
And ride on the wings of dreams
Of a gentler world.

271

Our faces are maps
Of the highway of deeds
We travel each day.

272

When night's sable hood
Smothers dusk's ashen embers
Saffron lamps twinkle.

273

The best remedy
For the blues is to whistle
The latest song hit.

274

A wink is useful
When seeking to intimate
Rather than define.

275

The Latin tango.
A dance that soon separates
Adults from children.

276

Word me a sentence
With elegant adjectives
That describes our love.

277

The good ship *Daydreams*
Weighs anchor each morning for
Its make-believe cruise.

278

In earlier times
War stressed the hate of people;
Today hate of war.

279

When people confer
Their unwritten agendas
Are of great import.

280

The Bible cites dogs
On several occasions;
But not ever cats.

281

There are no secrets.
If you tell one to a friend
He too has a friend.

282

Pilate's inquiry:
"What is truth?" always has vexed
The thinking of man.

283

If you can think it
There are words to express it;
No thought is nameless.

284

The greatest tyrants
With which all of us contend
Are ingrained habits.

285

Old Sacramento
Where serpentining rivers
Hold a rendezvous.

286

Mountains, streams and lakes;
Green trees and cherry blossoms,
Reveal Japan's soul.

287

Job retirement does
Not necessarily mean
Retirement from life.

288

Cobwebs do not form
In minds that constantly seek
The purpose of life.

289

In an argument
When one does not have the facts
He substitutes voice.

290

The cocktail party
Where all the guest talk in tongues
And no one listens.

291

Snow is impartial
It gives mansion and hovel
    The same white-spray job.

292

Earth's moon is *macho*
It never appears without
    Its masculine face.

293

Happy is the mind
That knows what to remember
And what to forget.

294

Fish are aquatics;
Torpedo shaped, cold blooded,
    Limbless and scaly.

295

Committee: The few
Who do the work for the group
    That gets the credit.

296

Birthdays measure the
Quantity of a life but
Not the quality.

297

Here for a moment
Seemingly significant —
Then oblivion.

298

Look to your actions;
Example is contagious
And imitated.

299

A shrinking planet
Demands leadership from those
With global vision.

300

Should one plant a tree
Even in drab surroundings
Singing birds will come.

301

The bruising rapids
Of life sometimes seem too rough
To permit passage.

302

He who hoards his life
Instead of expending it
Robs self and mankind.

303

Are we the products
Of all our relationships
With other people?

304

Man leads in the dance;
Woman's role is to fathom
His next direction.

305

When farewell time comes
And I step into the dark,
"Thank you," says it all.

Bibliography

Academic American Encyclopedia, Brolier, Inc., Danbury, Connecticut, 1984.

Asatori, Miyamori, *Haiku Poems,* Maruzen Co., Ltd., Tokyo, 1940.

The Encyclopedia Americana, International Edition, Brolier, Inc., Danbury, Connecticut, 1987.

Bukkyo Dendo Kyokai (Buddhist Promoting Foundation), *The Teaching of Buddha,* Printed by Kossaido Printing Co., Ltd., Tokyo, Japan, 1981.

The New Catholic Encyclopedia, Vol. VII, McGraw-Hill Co., New York, 1967.

The Concise Columbia Encyclopedia, Columbia University Press, New York, 1983.

The Crane's Bill, *Zen Poems of China and Japan,* Anchor Books, Doubleday, Garden City, New York, 1973.

The Standard Dictionary of Facts, Frontier Press, Buffalo, New York, 1916.

Henderson, Harold G., *The Bamboo Broom,* Houghton Mifflin Co., Boston, 1934.

Henderson, Harold G., *An Introduction to Haiku - An Anthology,* Doubleday, Garden City, New York, 1958.

Ichikawa, Sanki, *Haikai and Haiku,* Tokyo, Nippon, Gukajwtsu Shinkokai, 1958.

Keene, Donald, *From Japanese Literature, An Introduction For Western Readers,* Grove Press, Inc., New York, 1955.

Latourette, Kenneth Scott, *The History of Japan,* Macmillan, New York, 1947.

Noguchi, Yone, *The Spirit of Japanese Poetry*, J. Murray, London, 1914.

Stillman, Frances, *The Poets Manual and Rhyming Dictionary*, Thomas Y. Crowell, New York, 1965.

Stewart, Harold, *A Net of Fireflies —Japanese Haiku and Haiku Paintings*, Charles E. Tuttle Company, Publishers, Rutland, Vermont; Tokyo, Japan, 1960.

Stewart, Harold, *A Chime of Windbells, A Year of Japanese Haiku in English Verse, Translations With an Essay*. Charles E. Tuttle Company, Publishers, Rutland, Vermont; Tokyo, Japan, 1961.

Webster, Hutton, *History of the Far East*, D. C. Heath & Co., Boston, 1923.

Wood, Clement (Editor), *The Complete Rhyming Dictionary and Poet's Craft Book*, Doubleday and Company, Inc., Garden City, New York, 1936.

Wood, Clement, *Rhyming Dictionary (Unabridged)*, The World Publishing Company, New York, Sixteenth Printing, July, 1971.

Yasuda, Kenneth, *The Japanese Haiku, Its Essential Nature*, Charles E. Tuttle Company, Rutland, Vermont, 1958.

Author Silhouette

Born in California's capital, reared in railroad city Roseville, Placer County, Mel Lawson has viewed life from numerous vantage points. In high school and college, he was a student leader and athlete; in later life a teacher, administrator, naval officer, poet, composer, civic and fraternal spokesman. Indeed, he has served many people and numerous causes.

History long has been one of Lawson's interests. He has written *Saga of Service*, a history of the Rotary Club of Sacramento; *Flower Power*, the story of the Sacramento Camellia Festival; and was co-author of *Our America: Today and Yesterday*, a high school textbook.

His *October Roses*, a collection of twenty-one love songs testifies to his flair for music. His poem, "My Friend the Wind," was selected for a nationally published textbook for primary-grade children and shows the appeal of his poetry for youngsters as well as adults.

In his retirement years, Lawson frequently has expressed himself in verse, resulting in six books of poetry. Recently he became intrigued with the haiku, the subject of this, his seventh volume.

Lawson has received many citations for excellence, is a member of four honor societies, is listed in a number of Who's Who publications, and has had his verses appear in various anthologies.

He is a member of the California Writers Club, Sacramento Branch, and makes his home in Sacramento with his wife, Blanche.

Design: Teri Dugas, Sacramento, California
Typesetting: On the Ball Graphics, West Sacramento, California
Printing: Odyssey Press, Inc., Dover, New Hampshire